WITHDRAWN

U.S. Air Force Fighting Vehicles

ELLEN HOPKINS

Designed by Herman Adler Design
Photo research by Bill Broyles
Printed and bound in the United States by Lake Book
Manufacturing, Inc.

08 07 06 05
10 9 8 7 6 5 4 3 2

Library of Congress Cataloging-in-Publication Data

Hopkins, Ellen.
   U.S. Air Force fighting vehicles / by Ellen Hopkins.
      p. cm. -- (U.S. Armed Forces)
Summary: Provides an overview of the types of vehicles used
by the United States Air Force and their purposes.
Includes bibliographical references and index.
   ISBN 1-4034-0190-X (HC), 1-4034-0447-X (Pbk.)
   1. Airplanes, Military--United States--Juvenile literature.
2. Military helicopters--United States--Juvenile literature.
3. United States. Air Force--Weapons systems--Juvenile
literature. [1. Airplanes, Military. 2. Military helicopters.
3. Airplanes. 4. Helicopters. 5. United States. Air Force--
Weapons systems.] I. Title. II. U.S. Armed Forces (Series)
   UG1243.H67 2003
   623.7'46'0973--dc21

                                    2002015402

Acknowledgments
The author and publisher are grateful to the following for
permission to reproduce copyright material:
Cover courtesy of the United States Air Force
Title page, pp. 4, 6, 7, 8, 9, 10, 11, 12, 13, 14, 15, 16, 17,
18, 19, 20, 21, 22, 23, 24, 25, 26, 27, 28, 29, 30, 35, 36, 39,
41, 42, 43T Department of Defense; pp. 5, 31, 43C, 43B
United States Air Force; p. 32 Ellen Foster; p. 33 Roger
Ressmeyer/Corbis; p. 34 Jeff Kowalsky/AFP/Corbis; p. 37
Yann Arthus-Bertrand/Corbis; p. 38 Corbis SYGMA; p. 40
Lance H. Mayhew, Jr./AFP/Corbis

Special thanks to Lt. Col. G.A. Lofaro for his review of
this book.

Every effort has been made to contact copyright holders
of any material reproduced in this book. Any omissions
will be rectified in subsequent printings if notice is given
to the publisher.

Note to the Reader: Some words are shown in
bold, **like this.** You can find out what they mean
by looking in the glossary.

Contents

The Air Force Fleet

There are many types of aircraft in the United States Air Force's huge **fleet** of combat aircraft. There are fighters, bombers, transports, tankers, and helicopters. You can find them all at Nellis Air Force Base (AFB) in Nevada.

The U.S. Air Force's Weapons School at Nellis trains officers of the combat air forces. This is one of the top training schools in the world. The pilots and crews who train here learnto use the different types of air force planes and weapons.

Naming Aircraft

Aircraft are named using letters and numbers. The numbers are model numbers. The letters stand for the basic mission of the aircraft. A is used for attack planes. B is used for bombers. C is used for cargo (transport) planes. F is used for fighters. Helicopters have an H in their names, special mission planes have an M, and **tankers** have a K. **Reconnaissance** plane names use an E.

These planes have great power. They can turn quickly and more sharply than passenger planes. They can be flown blindly. This means that the pilot does not have to look outside the plane's windows to direct the plane. He or she only needs to look at the instruments in the **cockpit.**

An F-16 Fighting Falcon flies high above the earth.

F-15As from the 110th Fighter Squadron, 131st Fighter Wing, being piloted by members of the St. Louis Air National Guard.

These instruments provide information about how high the plane is and how sharply to turn it in order to change direction.

The planes can fly very fast. They are supersonic. This means they can fly faster than sound travels. In air, sound travels at about 750 miles (1,220 kilometers) per hour.

Earning Their Wings

Before U.S. Air Force pilots can fly combat missions, they must "earn their wings." First, they learn the basic skills all pilots must have. T aircraft are used for training. The air force's basic training airplane is the T-6 Texan II, a single-engine propeller plane. It is a **tandem-cockpit** airplane, which means the one pilot sits behind the other. It has an advanced **avionics** system. This plane can climb to 18,000 feet (5,476 meters) in less than six minutes.

After they learn how to fly the T-6 Texan II, pilots learn to fly jets. In twin-engine T-37B Tweets, students learn **formation** flying, night flying, and instrument flying. This jet gives student a feel for the even larger, faster jets that come next.

Know It

Avionics are electronic systems that aid flying. They include **radar, navigation,** and **communications** systems. Radar uses radio waves that are bounced off an object. Their echoes are measured, giving the object's size, location, and speed.

The T-37B Tweets is a jet aircraft used for training.

Test pilots and flight-test engineers are trained in T-38 Talons. In addition, the National Aeronautics and Space Administration (NASA) uses Talons to train astronauts and as chase planes for space shuttles.

Beyond basic jet training

After the jet plane part of the training, student pilots move on to one of four training areas, or tracks. The best students get to pick the tracks they want. These include the air force bomber-fighter track; the air force airlift-**tanker** or navy maritime track; the navy strike track; or the air force/navy helicopter track.

Students chosen for the bomber-fighter track train in the T-38A Talon. Talons are twin-engine, high-flying supersonic jets. Advanced students learn to fly the Talon in **aerobatics,** formation, night, instrument, and cross-country navigation training. They also train in the T-38B Talon. It has equipment that helps them learn how to aim the bombs and release them from the plane.

Those chosen to fly airlift or tanker aircraft receive training in the T-1A Jayhawk. This twin-engine plane can reach Mach 0.73. Instructor pilots also train in the T-1A. Jayhawk. Students who focus on navigation learn in T-43As. These are jets with high-tech navigation and communications equipment.

Bombs Away

The United States's first combat aircraft were bombers. They were created in 1911. These early **biplanes** belonged to the Aeronautical Division of the U.S. Army. There was no U.S. Air Force, yet. The planes were made of canvas, wood, and wire and open, or uncovered, cockpits. Pilots used charts, compasses, and luck to find their targets.

Conventional explosives get their power from the rapid burning of chemical compounds. Nuclear explosives get their power from splitting the core, or nucleus, of the **plutonium atom.** A baseball-sized ball of plutonium can create an explosion as big as 20,000 tons of conventional TNT.

Modern bombers

Today, bombers can fly across oceans without refueling, drop their bombs, and return home without stopping. Early in the Gulf War (1991), B-52 bombers took off from Barksdale AFB in Louisiana. They flew to Iraq combat zones, launched missiles, and came home. The 35-hour nonstop combat **sortie** took place on January 16, 1991. This mission, called Operation Secret Squirrel, was the first U.S. strike of the Gulf War.

B-52s

During Operation Enduring Freedom, B-52 bombers destroyed hundreds of enemy targets in Afghanistan. Once defense systems were defeated, **special operations** teams could safely go in to search for enemy forces.

The U.S. Air Force has used the B-52 for more than 40 years. It performs many missions. It is often used for ocean **surveillance,** helping the U.S. Navy in antiship and mine-laying operations. In two hours, two B-52s can cover 140,000 square miles (364,000 square kilometers) of ocean.

B-1 bombers fly lower and faster than B-52s and carry larger **payloads.** They have a swing wing design. The wings are in the forward position during takeoffs, landings, and during high-altitude flying.

B-1s have an **avionics** system that finds and deals with enemy **radar** threats. The system can also find missiles attacking the jets from behind. It defends the jet with countermeasures such as radar jamming and ejecting **chaff** and flares to confuse enemy missiles.

The B-1 bomber can detect missiles attacking from the rear. This plane has been painted in camouflage colors to make it harder to see.

Fearsome Fighters

In 1915, a German engineer put a machine gun with a timer on an airplane. This allowed the gun to be fired between the rotating **propellers.** This was the first fighter plane.

Modern fighter planes

Fighter planes today are much more advanced. The F-15 Eagle can perform better than any enemy aircraft. It can reach speeds of 1,875 miles (2,005 kilometers) per hour, and it can make tight turns without slowing down. The F-15 Eagle is used for combat in the air. Advanced **avionics** help it perform, too. A special **radar** system can find and track aircraft and small high-speed targets (such as missiles) as low as the treetops. The radar feeds information into a computer on the plane that automatically prepares the F-15's weapons.

F-15 Eagles take off.

The F-15 Eagle has eight air-to-air missiles to add to the firepower of its 20mm Gatling gun. An automated system lets the pilot fire these weapons with controls located on a control stick. The pilot can change from one weapons system to another.

The F-15E Strike Eagle is a fighter that can do two kinds of missions. It can be used for air-to-air and air-to-ground missions. It can fly into enemy territory, destroy ground targets, and fly back out, fighting the whole way.

The F-16 Fighting Falcon is another fighter that can do many things. It uses systems from the F-15 and older fighters. These were chosen and combined to make the jet simpler and smaller. Yet, despite its light weight, the F-16 is the only fighter aircraft that can withstand nine G's—nine times the force of gravity—with a full load of fuel.

An F-16 Eagle navigates through the sky.

Stealthy Birds

What is a stealth airplane? It cannot reach Mach 1 and it cannot make tight turns and other fancy moves in the air. An F-16 could easily outfly one. But its unique design and building materials makes it hard to see, with the eye or with **radar.** The word *stealth* means to move secretly.

The first plane that could avoid the enemy was the SR-71 Blackbird that first flew in 1964. The Blackbird flew so fast and so high on its **surveillance** missions, that the enemy could not shoot it down. It still holds the world records for speed, 2,193.167 miles (2345.15 kilometers) per hour, and altitude, 85,068.997 feet (25,929 meters). SR-71 Blackbirds were used for 24 years, but they were expensive to build and take care of.

During the Gulf War, F-117s flew over 1200 combat **sorties.** Without ever being hit by enemy gunfire, these fighters destroyed **communications** centers, bridges, railroads, highways, and storage facilities for nuclear and chemical weapons.

The B-2 Spirit bomber first flew combat missions in Operation Allied Force in Yugoslavia. The planes took off from Whiteman AFB in Missouri, and flew 30 hours without stopping. They attacked heavily defended targets in all weather conditions and returned safely.

In 1982, the F-117A Nighthawk was developed. The F-117A Nighthawk is a true stealth fighter. It is coated by a material that absorbs radar waves Its **faceted** shape (think diamonds) makes it difficult for ground radars to find it. It also has a special exhaust system, which reduces the heat from its engines. The F-117 does not engage in air-to-air combat. Instead, it sends **laser**-guided bombs in air-to-ground attacks.

The first B-2 Spirit bomber was made in 1988. It can operate alone or with very little support. Its long range lets it fly from bases in the United States to targets anywhere in the world without refueling. A large **payload** allows it to attack eight times more targets on a single mission than the F-117. The B-2 can carry a number of nuclear or regular weapons. It can attack heavily defended targets in any kind of weather.

A Is for Attack

In combat, attack aircraft and gunships provide support to people fighting on the ground. The first gunships were AC-47s. These were cargo planes that were changed so they could carry side-firing weapons. They were first used in the 1960s during the Vietnam War.

Then the military developed the AC-130 gunships and A-10 attack jets. They are very different. Like AC-47s, AC-130s are cargo planes that have been changed. They are huge and heavy. They also carry the most weapons of any fighting aircraft. Side-firing weapons can provide accurate air strikes for long periods, at night, and in bad weather.

The latest model of gunship is the AC-130U. It has advanced radars and **avionics** that can pinpoint targets from long distances. It can fire at two different targets at the same time, over half a mile (one kilometer) apart, using two different guns.

In Vietnam, AC-130 gunships destroyed more than 10,000 enemy vehicles. In Grenada (1983), they destroyed enemy defense systems. They have also provided close air support for troops in Iraq, Somalia, Bosnia, and Afghanistan.

The A-10 and OA-10 Thunderbolt IIs are the first U.S. Air Force planes made just to support ground troops. The light, quick, twin-engine jets were built to fly low and slowly, hit their targets, then escape quickly. They are easy to control at low altitudes and air speeds. Pilots and flight control systems are protected by **titanium** armor. These aircraft can be hit by armor-piercing and high explosive **projectiles**, almost 1 inch (23 millimeters) wide and keep on flying.

The Thunderbolt II has a 30mm Gatling gun attached to it. The gun can fire 3,900 rounds per minute, destroying many ground targets, including tanks and other vehicles. They also fire missiles.

The Warthog

The A-10 Thunderbolt II attack jet carries the most powerful gun ever placed on an aircraft. It is a cannon that fires milk-bottle-sized rounds at up to 3,900 shots every minute. The A-10 is designed to fly with an engine or even part of a wing shot completely off the plane. Its nickname is the Warthog.

Strategic Airlift

Strategic airlift uses cargo planes to transport combat units, **personnel**, equipment, and vehicles. They are delivered anywhere in the world even with less than a day to prepare. It is done with three cargo, or transport, aircraft: the C-141B, C-17, and C-5.

The C-141B Starlifter airlifts combat forces over long distances. It can land to deliver them, or the **paratroopers** can jump from the plane. It is also used for low-altitude drops of equipment. It can carry about 163 paratrooperess or up to 200 regular soldiers, depending on how many supplies are on the plane. The Starlifter can also carry over 100 patients and quickly transfer the sick and wounded from overseas to hospitals in the United States.

Know It

The C-141 was the first jet to airdrop paratroopers and the first to land in the Antarctic.

U.S. Air Force Transport

Other air force transport aircraft include

- the C-9 Nightingale, used mostly for medical evacuations
- the C-20, used to airlift high-ranking government officials
- the C-21, used for cargo and passenger airlift
- the C-22B, used by the Air National Guard to airlift **personnel**
- the C-32, a large airliner used by our nation's leaders, including the vice president and members of Congress
- the C-37, also used to airlift high-ranking government officials

The C-17 Globemaster III is the newest transport plane in the U.S. Air Force fleet. Its design allows it to use small, badly-equipped airfields, often near front lines. The C-17 Globemaster III can take off and land on short runways to deliver troops and heavy supplies.

The C-5 Galaxy is about as big as an aircraft gets. At 247 feet (75.3 meters) long and 65 feet (19.84 meters) high, the C-5 can carry 270,000 pounds (122,472 kilograms) of cargo. Air force C-5 Galaxies carry all of the army's combat equipment, including 74-ton mobile bridges, to combat areas around the world.

A C-17 Globemaster III can land on a runway that is only 3,000 feet (914 meters) long. Most passenger jets of the same size need about two times as much space, or even more.

Flying Feast

C-17 Globemaster III aircraft has been used to deliver food to poverty-stricken areas in times of war. This **humanitarian** aid helps innocent citizens who might be trapped by the fighting.

Hercules Knockoffs

The C-130 Hercules is another type of cargo plane. It performs **tactical** airlift missions. The C-130 is the plane used most often to airdrop troops and equipment into enemy areas. It can carry oversized cargo, including helicopters and armored vehicles. It can also drop loads up to 42,000 pounds (19,050 kilograms). This aircraft's design allows it to be used for many different kinds of missions. Specialized versions are used to fly supplies to the Arctic, for medical missions, on weather **reconnaissance,** to fight fires, and for natural disaster relief.

The AC-130 gunship is a C-130 Hercules that has been changed, or modified. The HC-130 is also a modified C-130. It is a long-range aircraft. The HC-130 refuels search-and-rescue helicopters and airdrops **pararescue** teams, rubber boats, or other equipment that might help survivors until rescue vehicles can reach them.

An LC-130, a special C-130 used for polar missions, awaits **deployment** to Antarctica as part of Operation Deep Freeze. This joint operation of the U.S. armed forces and the New Zealand Defense Forces supports the U.S. National Science Foundation's Antarctic Program.

The WC-130's Omega Dropsonde Windfinding System (ODWS) is used to track hurricanes.

The EC-130H Compass Call is another modified C-130 Hercules. It uses an electronic system called Rivet Fire to interrupt, or jam, enemy **communications.** The EC-130H usually supports air operations. It can also provide support to ground force operations by jamming enemy communications.

The WC-130 is flown by the Air Force Reserve for weather reconnaissance missions. These missions usually last eleven hours. The plane covers around 3,500 miles (3,742.5 kilometers). The crew collects and reports weather information every minute.

Instruments on the aircraft measure temperature, humidity, wind speed, and wind direction. This information, along with additional information collected by the crew, is sent by satellite to the National Weather Service's National Hurricane Center in Miami, Florida.

Hovering

The first helicopter that flew was named H-1. Construction of the H-1 began in July, 1921. In December 1922, a helicopter carrying Major Thurman H. Bane, of the U. S. Air Service, rose 6 feet (2 meters) in the air. It stayed there for 1 minute and 42 seconds. The H-1 was hard to control, and the air force worked to improve their helicopters.

Hawks and Hueys

Today's HH-60G Pave Hawk is the air force's main helicopter. Its main mission is to rescue downed aircrew or other **personnel.** In peacetime, its missions include **civil** search and rescue, medical evacuations, disaster relief, antidrug operations, and NASA space shuttle support.

Unlike the first H-1, the HH-60G has excellent control. On rescue missions, the HH-60G can lift a 600-pound (270-kilogram) load while hovering only 200 feet (60.7 meters) above the ground.

There are two main types of night-vision technology. One type makes light seem brighter, producing the green-screen effect shown here. Without this system, at night a pilot might not see a person only 30 feet (9 meters) away. With night vision, a pilot could see someone 1,740 feet (530 meters) away. Forward-looking infrared technology uses an invisible light beam to "see.".

The HH-60G Pave Hawk is a modified, or changed, army Black Hawk helicopter. It has a night-vision system and global positioning and satellite **communications** systems. HH-60G Pave Hawks carry two 7.62mm machine guns.

The air force also uses UH-1N Hueys. These helicopters are used for many light-duty missions, including medical evacuations, search-and-rescue, and visitor transport.

Know It

The Global Positioning System (GPS) shows the user's exact position on Earth anytime, anywhere, in any weather. Twenty-four GPS satellites send signals that can be detected by anyone with a GPS receiver. With the receiver, a person can find out his or her exact location.

A crew member on a ship guides a UH-1N Huey Medical Evacuation helicopter about to land on the deck.

Missions Impossible

U. S. Air Force special operations forces sometimes perform dangerous missions behind enemy lines. The aircraft that support them have an *M* in their names for mission. M-series aircraft go in and out of enemy territory quickly and quietly, often under cover of darkness.

The MH-53J Pave Low III heavy lift helicopter is the best helicopter in the U.S. Air Force fleet. It is used for low-**altitude,** long range, secret invasions of enemy territory. Day or night, bad weather or good, the MH-53J Pave Low III delivers special operations forces to their missions. It takes supplies to them and picks them up when their mission is complete. To accomplish its dangerous work, the MH-53J Pave Low III has a special **navigation** system. It tracks the land below and makes a map.

▲ An MH-53J Pave Low III prepares to land on the deck of a ship during exercises.

The MC-130P Combat Shadow provides air refueling for special operations helicopters.

It is the job of the MC-130P Combat Shadow to refuel MH-53J Pave Low IIIs. The MC-130P Combat Shadow may also bring special operations forces to enemy territory. To perform this mission, it usually flies at night, without lights or **communications** to avoid enemy **radar**. The cres uses night-vision goggles to see.

The MC130E and H Combat Talon I and II also deliver, pick up, and resupply special operations teams. They can also refuel helicopters in enemy territory. These planes have a special electronic system that lets crews find and avoid dangers. The MC130E and H Combat Talon I and II may also drop bombs and leaflets. The leaflets try to convince enemy troops to surrender.

Mission Accomplished

In April 1996, air force special operations troops helped evacuate more than 2,000 people from Monrovia, Liberia, in Africa during Operation Assured Response. MH-53 Pave Lows picked up people at the American embassy in Monrovia and flew them to Sierra Leone. There, they met MC-130 Combat Talon II aircraft for a flight to Dakar, Senegal. Supporting the operation were AC-130 Spectre gunships and HC-130P Combat Shadow **tankers**.

Midair Refueling

Modern combat aircraft often must fly thousands of miles before they reach their targets. Once they get there, pilots do not want to risk a dangerous landing to refuel. A U.S. Air Force tanker is an airborne filling station. It supplies fuel for air force aircraft and also for aircraft used by the navy, marine corps, and friendly nations as well.

Tankers are named using the letter *K*. The KC-135 Stratotanker is basically a 707 passenger plane. It has giant fuel tanks instead of seats inside. These tanks can hold 200,000 pounds (90,719 kilograms) of fuel. When an aircraft needs more fuel, a crew person near the back of the KC-135 Stratotanker lowers a boom. The boom actss as a long gas pipe. Fuel passes through the pipe to supply the aircraft that needs it.

The KC-10A Extender is also a modified passenger plane. Its basic form is the DC-10. This aircraft can combine the jobs of a tanker and a transport plane. It can refuel fighters while carrying **personnel** and equipment.

A K-10A Extender refuels a B-2 Spirit Bomber aircraft.

The KC-10A Extender uses either a boom or a hose and drogue system. A drogue is like a large funnel attached to the end of a gas hose. The KC-10A Extender can refuel many different kinds of aircraft on the same mission.

A KC-135 Stratotanker prepares to refuel four F-16 Falcon aircraft. The boom can be seen at the back of the KC-135.

Specialized Transports

Like the C-130 Hercules, the C-135 has different versions that have many different roles.

One role of C-135 aircraft is to transport senior military **personnel.** But the C-135C Speckled Trout tests **communications** technologies. For one test, an antenna system was put on the plane. It then successfully received satellite-transmitted television signals and other information. This new system lets a commander keep watch over a battlefield, while communicating with important operations centers.

The NKC-135 Big Crow is a flying laboratory. It is used for testing electronic warfare equipment. The NKC-135 Big Crow can also jam enemy **radar** systems and perform other electronic tasks.

The EC-135 used to be the U.S. Strategic Command's flying command post. The mission was called Looking Glass. One EC-135 was always on alert. For almost 30 years, one EC-135 was always in the air, 365 days a year, 24 hours a day. If ground control

This EC-135 Stratotanker is flown by the 10th Airborne Command Control Squadron. The Stratotanker's main mission is air-to-air refueling.

This is an OC-135B Open Skies aircraft.

of U.S. bombers or missiles became lost, this aircraft would take command. In 1998, the navy took over the Looking Glass mission and the EC-135 was no longer used.

One world, one sky

The OC-135B Open Skies flies unarmed observation flights in support of the Open Skies Treaty. This treaty allows all the countries who signed it to gather information about military forces and activities that concern them. Four cameras mounted at the back of the aircraft take photos. A recording system labels each photo with the aircraft's position and **altitude**, plus the time and other information. This information is recorded and downloaded onto a computer disk.

Know It

The Open Skies Treaty allows short-notice, unrestricted observation flights over each country that signed the treaty. As of January 1, 2002, 27 countries, including the United States, have signed the treaty.

Spying from High Above

The U-2 Dragon Lady flies so high that no enemy will find it. It is the U.S. Air Force's first and only manned high-**altitude** spy plane. It supports both U.S. and allied forces (forces from friendly countries). Extra-long wings make the U-2 look a bit like a glider. But this also makes takeoffs and landings very difficult. Because the U-2 reaches altitudes of over 70,000 feet (21,341 meters), pilots must use a full-pressure suit that is similar to the suits that astronauts wear.

Know It

At 70,000 feet (21,341 meters), pilots wear special suits that make the pressure inside and outside their bodies the same.

The U-2 uses technology to learn about small or full-scale conflicts. High-tech sensors and **radars** form images and send them to stations on the ground for study. U-2s also gather information about natural disasters and test the air for NASA.

The U-2 gathers information by "seeing" what is happening. Another plane, called the RC-135 Rivet Joint, gathers information by "listening," or eavesdropping on electronic signals. It finds enemy forces and discovers

U-2 Dragon Lady

If a U-2 Dragon Lady flight goes well, it is characterized as "dancing with the lady." If it goes poorly, pilots say they "fought with the dragon."

what they are going to do. Then, it passes that information to ground troops or other aircraft. The RC-135 Rivet Joint usually works together with an airborne warning and control system (AWACS) and Joint **Surveillance** Target Attack Radar System (Joint STARS).

The E-3 Sentry is another type of spy plane. It is a modified Boeing 707. It has a large radar system that can look at all of Earth, over land or water. It collects information on aircraft and ships so commanders on the ground know their location, direction, and speed.

While the E-3 Sentry looks at the sea and sky, the E-8C Joint STARS observes battlefields. This plane's radar and computer systems gather detailed information about ground troops. Its job is to identify land targets.

The E-3 Sentry uses radar to collect information about battleships and other aircaft.

Where Pilots Dare Not Fly

If it is too dangerous to send pilots into an area, the U.S. Air Force will use planes operated by remote control (there is no pilot). There are two of these aircraft: the RQ-1 Predator and the Global Hawk.

The RQ-1 Predator is more than just an aircraft flown by remote control. It is a complete system with sensors, a ground control station, and a Predator satellite link. A pilot and two sensor operators sit side-by-side on the ground and run the plane. They watch two television screens.

One screen shows important information such as **altitude**, speed, and angle of attack. The other screen shows a map of the target area. A symbol on the screen is used for the Predator. As in playing a video game, the pilot's right hand uses a control stick to control the aircraft. Commands are sent to the Predator by radio and satellite.

Workers check an RQ-1 Predator before a flight demonstration.

The R in RQ-1 stands for **reconnaissance.** The Q means unmanned aircraft system. The 1 means it is the first model built.

In April 2001, the Global Hawk flew nonstop to Australia, a distance of 7,500 miles (12,000 kilometers). It set a record for unmanned aircraft.

The RQ-1 Predator can fly as high as 25,000 feet (7,620 meters) or as low as 10,000 feet (3,000 meters). That is low enough to pick out people on the ground and identify what they're wearing. Yet because it is small (only 27 feet or about 8 meters long) and white, it is hard to see in the sky. **Radar** can pick it up, but since it flies at low speeds (as do small civilian aircraft), most radars screen it out.

The Global Hawk is the air force's newest remote-controlled aircraft. It flies up to 65,000 feet (20,000 meters) high and can reach speeds of 400 miles (644 kilometers) per hour. Global Hawk looks at large areas and gives the most up-to-date information about enemy resources and movements.

Unlike the Predator, Global Hawk can take off, fly its mission, return, and land on its own. It is programmed with this information before it leaves the ground. Operators on the ground keep track of it and can change the flight plan while the Global Hawk is in the air.

Walk with Agent Teeia Phillips

Special agent Teeia [pronounced TEE-ah] Phillips makes sure the companies that build aircraft for the air force build them right. Like all members of the Air Force Office of Special Investigations (AFOSI), Phillips's mission is to keep American fighters safe. If the jets are not safe, then the fighters are not safe. Phillips's office is in Atlanta, Georgia, but she covers five states, looking for procurement fraud.

Phillips joined the air force after she finished high school. After working as a **personnel** specialist in Turkey, Korea, and Virginia, she cross-trained as an AFOSI agent. "I decided to leave active duty but stayed in the reserves. I work for AFOSI as a civilian."

> Procurement fraud is when a person or company substitutes poor-quality products or services for the better ones they have promised to provide. Quality-control experts are company representatives who are supposed to keep that from happening.

Phillips has an office at Lockheed Martin, the Department of Defense's main aircraft builder. "We contract with companies like Lockheed and Boeing to build airplanes a certain way for a certain number of dollars," she explained. "One of my jobs is to make sure they don't substitute inferior parts, which cost less but could be dangerous. You wouldn't want them to build jets with bolts that are a little too small, for instance. Yes, it has happened, and yes, it's a crime."

↑ Teeia Phillips at work for the OSI.

This B-1 bomber is being built in California. AFOSI agents make sure the job is done right.

If Phillips suspects a problem, an investigation is started. It can take at least a year, often longer. Phillips walks along assembly lines, looking at parts and talking to workers. She talks to quality-control experts. She reads and rereads contracts. Reading a contract is not easy to do.

"The contract for the F-22 Raptor is bigger than my living room," she said, not joking at all. Sometimes she finds mistakes. Other times she finds that a contract has been changed since it was first written.

Should Phillips decide a "mistake" was done on purpose, it is a crime. She reports it to the U.S. Attorney General's office. If there is enough evidence, the office will file charges. "Usually, the company settles out of court," she said, meaning they will pay a heavy fine. "No one wants a long, expensive trial. But we do want the problems to be corrected."

In Orbit

It might surprise you to know how many artificial satellites orbit Earth right now. Some satellites help forecast weather. **Surveillance** satellites monitor military activity. **Navigation** satellites pinpoint the location of objects on Earth. **Communications** satellites carry radio, telephone, or television signals long distances. The Air Force Space Command (AFSC) is in charge of many satellites.

Eyes in the Sky

A satellite is any object moving around a star or planet. Our moon, which revolves around Earth, is a satellite. An artificial satellite is any man-made object placed in orbit around a star or planet. Since the first artificial satellite was launched in 1957, thousands of "man-made moons" have circled Earth.

Some air force satellites provide information to everyone. The Global Positioning System (GPS) gives navigation information to anyone with a GPS receiver. The Defense Meteorological Satellite Program (DMSP) collects and gives out global weather information.

U.S. Staff Sergeant Juna Coba looks at a computer displaying GPS information.

Private viewing

Other air force satellites send **encrypted** data that only special receivers can decode. The Defense Satellite Communications System (DSCS) is ten satellites that orbit about 22,000 miles (35,200 kilometers) out in space. These satellites send voice, data, and television signals between military sites. Milstar is a communications system. It has four grouped satellites that act like a telephone switchboard. It directs communications from anywhere in the world.

The U.S. Air Force Defense Support Program (DSP) is a key part of North America's early warning systems. These satellites can detect heat from missiles against Earth's background. This indicates enemy missile launches, space launches, or nuclear explosions. AFSC units report such information, by satellite, to early warning centers at Cheyenne Mountain, near Colorado Springs, Colorado. These centers immediately forward the information to "need-to-know" agencies around the world.

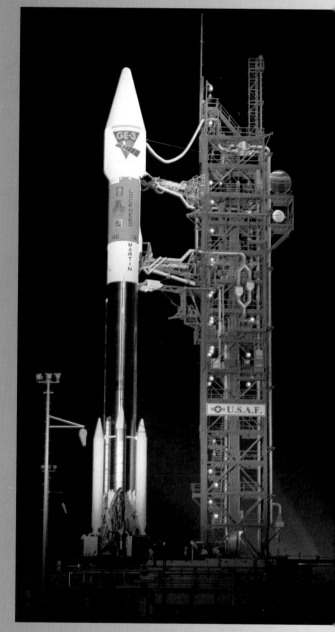

Rocket launch

This Atlas IIA rocket is ready to launch at Cape Canaveral, Florida. It is carrying a communications satellite. The Atlas project began in the early 1960s. An Atlas booster carried astronaut John Glenn into orbit for Project Mercury, the first U.S. manned space program. Atlas space launch vehicles were also used in all three manned mooned missions.

Going Ballistic

Intercontinental ballistic missiles (ICBMs) are weapons armed with nuclear warheads. Yet they are designed to prevent war. Few nations want to risk nuclear warfare. The U.S. plan to prevent war is based on three kinds of weapons. They are long range bombers armed with nuclear missiles, submarine-launched ballistic missiles (SLBM), and ICBMs.

The Peacekeeper is the United States's newest ICBM. It can send ten warheads to ten different targets. Four rockets launch, or boost, the missile into space. The top section, called the post-boost vehicle, separates from the rockets and turns toward its target area. Once it has safely re-entered the atmosphere, the cone-shaped warheads are released. Each follows a ballistic path to its target.

An LG-118A Peacekeeper intercontinental missile is tested. Peacekeeper missiles like these are the United States' most advanced nuclear weapons. However, new bunker-busting nuclear weapons called earth penetrators are being planned.

This is the view from inside a missile silo.

The U.S. Air Force has 500 Minuteman ICBMs on air bases in Wyoming, Montana, and North Dakota. They are protected by hardened silos, or bins, and are connected by cables to underground launch-control centers. Launch crews are on alert at all times. Orders to launch would come from the national command authorities in ground-based control centers. If ground **communication** is lost, an E-6B airborne launch-control center aircraft would assume command.

Know It

Ballistic missiles follow an arching, or ballistic, path, like that of a baseball when it is thrown. A rocket blasts the missile onto a planned course and shuts off. The missile coasts, then falls on target.

Sidewinders and Harpoons

The air force often uses a number of nonballistic missiles. Cruise missiles fly at heights of about 50 feet (15 meters). They have a range of up to 2,000 miles (3,200 kilometers). These missiles use computerized maps to locate their targets.

Cruise missiles can be launched from ships or from the ground. The air force launches its AGM-86Bs (nuclear) and AGM-86Cs (regular) from B-52 planes. Each aircraft can carry twenty missiles. Enemy forces have to attack each missile, making defense difficult.

The AGM-88 HARM (high speed anti-radiation missile) is an air-to-surface missile that finds and destroys enemy air defense systems. They are carried only by F-16 fighter jets.

Know It

Pulse Doppler **radar** tracks an object's speed. This is what police officers use to measure the speed of an automobile.

This GBU-10 Pavweway II is an example of a laser-guided missile. (This type is used by the navy.)

The AGM-84D Harpoon is an antiship missile. Originally developed for the U.S. Navy, Harpoons were also used by B-52s. The bombers carry eight Harpoons on the outside of the aircraft. Inside, the B-52s can carry sea mines. Armed with Harpoons and mines, the B-52s give U.S. naval forces total control of targeted waters.

Know It

Nonballistic missiles are powered for their entire flight. They fall into four main categories: air-to-air, air-to-surface, surface-to-surface, and surface-to-air.

Fighter aircraft carry the AIM-9 Sidewinder. This is a heat-seeking air-to-air missile. It flies at supersonic speeds. A sensor "looks" for heat from an enemy aircraft's exhaust to locate the target. This lets pilots fire the missile and then escape while the missile guides itself to the target.

This AIM-9 Sidewinder air-to-air missile is being loaded on to a navy F/A-18C Hornet on an aircraft carrier. The air force also uses these missiles.

Smart Weapons

Precision-guided weapons are "smart" in a couple of ways. In the daytime, they use television cameras to locate targets. At night, or when the weather is bad, **infrared** video or **lasers** are used.

The AGM-65 Maverick is a precision-guided air-to-surface missile. It is used mostly for antitank or antiship missions. It can also be used against other ground targets, including **radars** or fuel-storage places. The Maverick is a **modular** weapon. Different combinations of warheads can be attached to the rocket to make different weapons.

Maverick A/Bs are guided by a television system. What the system sees will appear on a TV screen in the cockpit. The pilot chooses his or her target, locks on, then launches the missile. The infrared Maverick D can also track heat created by a target. This gives the pilot a video display at night or in cloudy weather.

AGM-65 Mavericks ready to be loaded. The air force first received AGM Mavericks in 1972. The Maverick As are no longer used.

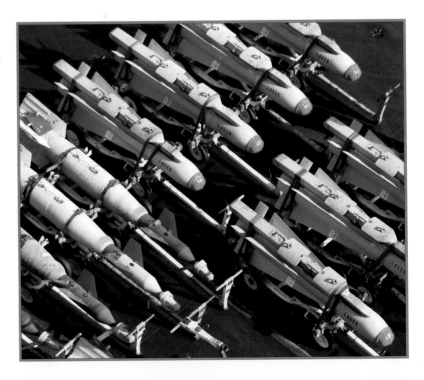

The GBU-15 can be used for direct or indirect attacks.

The GBU-15 is a modular weapon used to destroy important enemy targets. The guidance system, either television or infrared, attaches to the nose of the warhead. In a direct attack, the pilot chooses the target, locks on, and launches the weapon. In an indirect attack, the pilot releases the weapon, then looks for the target. Once it is located, the pilot directs the weapon by remote control.

Educated Bombs
The Joint Direct Attack Munitions (JDAM) is a kit that changes unguided free-fall bombs into accurate, poor-weather "smart" bombs.

The Paveway series of GBUs uses laser-guided systems. They are the best weapons to use against small, well-defended targets. This technology allows more hits with far fewer missions and fewer aircraft. Targets can also be hit from greater distances.

Air Power Tomorrow

The United States Air Force will always need the very best fighting vehicles technology has to offer. Several new vehicles are being designed and others are being tested to make sure they will perform well.

One of these is the F-22 Raptor. It will replace the F-15 in 2004. The F-22 has a stealth design. It has supersonic speed and is easy to control. It has other advantages over the F-15:

- The F-22 Raptor reflects a **radar** signal about the size of a bumblebee. The best enemy defense systems cannot detect it.

- The F-22 Raptor is the first fighter that can fly at Mach 1.5 without using afterburners, which can increase a jet's power but use a lot of fuel. Therefore, the F-22 Raptor is more efficient.

- The F-22 Raptor uses more advance weapons.

The new Joint Strike Fighter (JSF) will complement the F-22 Raptor. The JSF is a single fighter plane that will be used by the U.S. Air Force, Navy, and Marines. and Great Britain's Royal Air Force and Navy.

An F-22 Raptor performs difficult maneuvers.

You can see the airplane wings and the helicopter rotors on this MV-22 Osprey Tilt Rotor helicopter.

Another new aircraft is the CV-22. It will be used by Air Force **Special Operations** teams. The CV-22 Osprey looks like a combination of an airplane and a helicopter. It can take off, hover (stay in one place in the air), and land like a helicopter. Once airborne, the engine and prop-rotors on each wing rotate forward and it can fly like a plane. The Osprey has twice the speed, range, and **payload** of the MH-53 Pave Lows now used by special operations teams.

A new unmanned aerial vehicle will be tested until 2005. The X-45A Unmanned Combat Air Vehicle (UCAV) has an unusual design. At only 27 feet (8.23 meters) long, it can be taken apart and stored in a small container and then be rebuilt in about an hour.

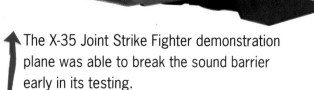

The X-35 Joint Strike Fighter demonstration plane was able to break the sound barrier early in its testing.

The X-45 UCAV's mission will be combat. These vehicles will go in and destroy enemy defenses before ground troops arrive. But they will do it without putting pilots in danger.

The UCAVs design and small size almost make it look like a model airplane.

Nose to Tail: How Air Force Aircraft Measure Up

Helicopters

	Length	Height	Diameter of Rotors
MH-53J Pave Low III	88'	25'	72'
HH-60G Pave Hawk	64'8"	16'8"	53'7"
UH1-N Huey	57'3"	12'9"	Main: 48' Tail: 8'6"

Transport

	Length	Height	Wingspan
C-130E/H/J	97'9"	38'3"	132'7"
C-141B	168'4"	39'3"	160'
C-17	174'	55'1"	169'10"
C-5	247'1"	65'1"	222'9"

Jets

	Length	Height	Wingspan
F-16	49'5"	16'	32'8"
F-15	63'8"	18'5"	42'8"
F-117A (Stealth)	65'9"	12'9"	43'4"
A-10	53'4"	14'8"	57'6"
B-2 (Stealth)	69'	17'	172'
B-1	146'	34'	137' (wings forward)
B-52	159'4"	40'8"	185'
U-2	63'	16'	103'

Miscellaneous

	Length	Height	Wingspan
KC-135 Stratotanker	136'3"	41'8"	130'10"
E-3 (AWACS)	145'6"	41'4"	130'10"
RQ-1 Predator	27'	6'9"	48'7"

Glossary

aerobatics flying moves, such as rolling and diving

altitude height

avionics electronic systems in planes, such as radar and communications

biplane airplane with two wings on each side, one above the other

chaff metal foil dropped by aircraft to confuse enemy radar

civil not military

cockpit place where the plane's pilot sits

communications sharing information

deployment to send into battle

emission waste material, usually a gas, given off by a vehicle

encrypted in code

faceted having a number of flat surfaces

formation an organized pattern

humanitarian helpful to people

infrared invisible rays of light that can be sensed because they give off heat

laser invisible, high-energy beam of light

modular built with pieces that can be changed for other pieces

navigation finding out where something is and find the directions to get to it

pararescue person who has medical training and parachutes from an airplane to reach wounded soldiers

paratrooper soldier that jumps from planes to reach his or her target

payload weight carried by an aircraft or vehicle; the warhead of a missile

personnel people

plutonium metallic chemical element that is used as an energy source

projectile object which that be thrown or shot , such as stones or bullets

radar invisible waves of energy bounced off an object find it

reconnaissance look at or explore something to get information about it

rudder movable piece of an aircraft wing, used for right/left steering

sortie flight mission

special operations soldiers with special training who sometimes perform secret missions

strategic made or trained to destroy enemy bases behind the lines of battle

surveillance watch and listen

tactical organized or used for action against enemy troops

tandem one behind the other

tilt rotor helicopter blade, called a rotor that tilts instead of being only in the vertical position over the helicopter

titanium strong, lightweight metal used to make steel

More Books to Read

George, Linda, and Charles George. *The Tuskegee Airmen.* Danbury, Conn.: Children's Press, 2001.

Reavis, Tracey. *Stealth Jet Fighter: The F-117A.* Danbury, Conn.: Children's Press, 2000.

Sweetman, Bill. *Combat Rescue Helicopters: The MH-53 Pave Lows.* Mankato, Minn.: Capstone Press, 2002.

A Place to Visit

United States Air Force Museum, 1100 Spaatz St., Wright-Patterson Air Force Base Dayton, OH 45433, phone: (937) 255-3286
www.wpafb.af.mil/museum/index.htm

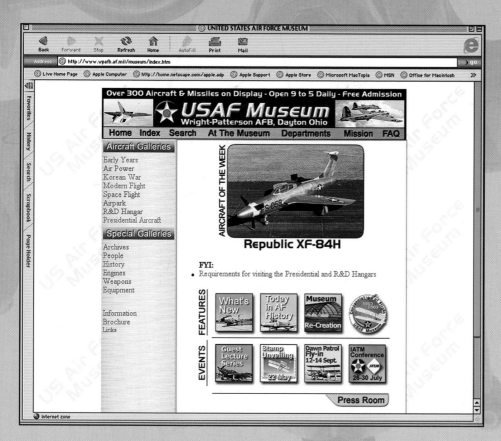

Index